Quilt Care, Construction and Use Advice

How to Help Your Quilt Live to 100

Full-color Edition

BARB GORGES

CHEYENNE, WYOMING

Cover: These three quilts, circa 1890-1920, are still in our family and in decent shape. We aren't sure if our great-grandmother made them—there are no signatures. We only know that they came from the William A. Witte family dairy farm outside Madison, Wisconsin

Copyright © 2017 by Barb Gorges. All rights reserved.
Photographs, except as noted, copyrighted by the author.

Published by Yucca Road Press
3417 Yucca Road, Cheyenne, Wyoming 82001

Yucca Road Press logo drawn by Jane Dorn of Lingle, Wyoming and designed by Chris Hoffmeister, Western Sky Design, Cheyenne, Wyoming.

ISBN 978-0-9992945-3-6

Full-color print edition, August 2020

This book is based on blog posts by the author previously published at GorgesQuiltLabels.com and in the Wyoming State Quilt Guild newsletter between 2014 and 2017.

Dedicated to my family,
all of whom appreciate and value quilts.

Table of Contents

Introduction.........................1
Chapter 1 – Make 4
Chapter 2 – Test 10
Chapter 3 – Use....................13
Chapter 4 – Display.................16
Chapter 5 – Air 19
Chapter 6 – Wash 21
Chapter 7 – Dry....................25
Chapter 8 – Store..................27
Chapter 9 – Appraise................30
Chapter 10 – Insure.................32
Chapter 11 – Ship 34
Chapter 12 – Sign 37
Acknowledgements 41
Resources..........................43
Index 45
Author 47

Introduction

For a quilt, love looks like frayed fabrics.

What can we do to help quilts last longer? Longevity has two factors, nature and nurture. For people, this translates into genetics and lifestyle.

The same can be said for quilts. "Genetic" factors that promote long quilt life are good quality materials and good construction techniques.

A healthy lifestyle for quilts means owners follow good care and use practices and avoid accidents.

This book has information on how we can help our quilts live to 100, whether we made the quilts ourselves or acquired them.

What can we do to help our quilts when we, or this book, aren't around—whether we are merely away from home or whether we've given our quilts to someone else?

Thirty-five years ago, I was making lots of quilted pillows and placemat sets (hand quilted!) for friends and relatives getting married or graduating, and I wasn't sure they would know how to wash them safely.

I made "hang tags" out of cardstock, writing out washing directions and pinning them to the gifts. You can imagine as soon as the recipient unpinned them, the directions were not filed by the washing machine. So instead I started printing brief care directions at the bottom of each fabric documentation label.

Printing with permanent ink on fabric, no matter how fine the pen, takes a lot of room. But one day I said "Eureka!" when I realized a solution had already been invented. Care labels are in our clothes and on our linens. Why not make one for home-made quilts?

I found a company that wove taffeta labels and had them produce one with the basic quilt care information. I was going to make enough for me, but there was a good price break at 10,000 and so I went into business.

Between 1998 and 2016, I distributed 97,000 Gorges Quilt Care Labels in all 50 states and three other countries. I am surprised the labels didn't sell better. Perhaps it was because quilters don't need them until they finish a quilt—and you know how many unfinished quilts we all have!

Maybe quilters have faith that the person receiving the quilt will know how to take care of it. Really? There are so many stories about handmade quilts inadvertently ruined by the recipient.

My customers were putting the quilt care labels on quilts they gave away. But why not put them on quilts in our own house? We aren't always at home when the cat throws up on the prize-winning quilt on our bed and a family member or the house sitter decides to wash the quilt before we get home. We'll improve chances of success if we have washing instructions on our quilt.

Back when I was developing the care label, I asked Laramie, Wyoming, antique quilt guru Anne Olsen to review the text and she wrote a three-page letter with all the information I hadn't included on the label. There is more to quilt care than washing instructions.

For several years, I gave presentations to guilds in Colorado, Nebraska and Wyoming about "How to Help Your Quilts Live to 100." I brought examples of the many ways quilts age prematurely such as vintage quilts folded perfectly in half decade after decade, or my own quilts made with fabrics incompatible with the thread they were sewn with.

The most important steps we can take for the future well-being of our quilts are those that show we value them. Putting care information on a quilt is one way to indicate to the next owner that the quilt is valuable enough to take the time to add it.

Label your quilt. Add information about when, where and why the quilt was made. If you've ever had a vintage quilt appraised, you know it is more valuable if there is information about the quilter and the quilt, so label your quilts for the sake of your heirs. You might not be around to hand the quilt to them.

Provide a cloth bag or cloth wrapping for when the quilt is stored, to protect it from dust or touching the raw wood of a cedar chest or shelf.

Provide a certified appraisal of the quilt's value and impress your heirs. Perhaps it will help them treasure your quilt more.

Make a beautiful quilt that appeals to people so they want to keep it, even if you just want to use up scraps to make a warm layer for your spare bed.

For those of us who care about quilts as an art form and a means of self-expression, the worst fate for a quilt is to be used harshly in a way we didn't intend—such as moving van padding or dog's bed. A natural disaster would be less painful.

On the other hand, perhaps our quilts have been made to swaddle a baby, comfort the bereaved or warm our loved ones. If they have been loved to pieces, what more could we ask?

Barb Gorges
Cheyenne, Wyoming
February 22, 2017

Gorges Quilt Care Labels were available 1998-2016.

Chapter 1 - Make

Disintegrated fabric patch leaves nothing behind but the stitches.

The longevity of a quilt depends not only on the care it receives, but on the quality of its fabric and other materials. Spend some time with old bed quilts and you will see how a quilter's choices play out.

Fabric

My mother found and gave me an old, well-worn double nine-patch scrap quilt that was made with a collection of all kinds of fabrics, everything from a little bit of terrycloth to filmy chiffon. The less hardy weaves (and knits) had disintegrated and the batting was fluffing out in many places. But the plain "quilting" cottons were wearing their age well.

If you are going to make an important bed quilt, you'll want to buy best quality fabric so that it ages well, putting off the day it might be relegated to picnics.

How do you find good fabric? In general, we figure the big box stores have seconds and quilt shops have top quality. However, once in a great while I've been lucky at Wal-Mart and unlucky at a quilt shop.

There are two ways I judge fabric quality: the fabric itself, and the color.

Spend a lot of time at quilt shops and feel the expensive fabric. It has a good thread count—though not so much that the fabric feels stiff. Batiks have a much tighter weave, or higher thread count, than regular quilting cottons, but they are flexible. Good fabric isn't too thin and it isn't as thick as broadcloth. Thick or high thread count fabric like batik is difficult to hand quilt (does anyone hand quilt anymore?). Thin fabric won't wear well.

Too much finish can be added to fabric. I've bought nice, crisp fabric—great for piecing, but it never relaxed in the wash. Sometimes a stiff finish washes out and has been hiding a light-weight fabric you would not have otherwise purchased.

Quality color printing is the other important aspect. In a multi-colored print, colors are printed separately and need to register, or line up, correctly. Are those flower centers supposed to be set in some abstract design a quarter-inch away from the center of the circle of petals? Look at those dots on the selvedge. Each little circle (some companies use more creative shapes) in the row should be filled perfectly with one of the colors printed. There may be some extra circle outlines if a print doesn't have a lot of different colors.

Watch out for prints that feel like they are painted on. I ordered a red nightgown with white polka dots and when I received it, I realized I could feel each dot, as if I could pick it off with my fingernail. Over time, color applied this way, instead of dyed into the fibers, will crack.

All those luscious prints sparkling with gold highlights have a similar problem. I used a navy blue fabric printed with gold stars in a quilt for a son who used it every night for more than 10 years. The stars tarnished, adding to the wonderful patina of wear and love.

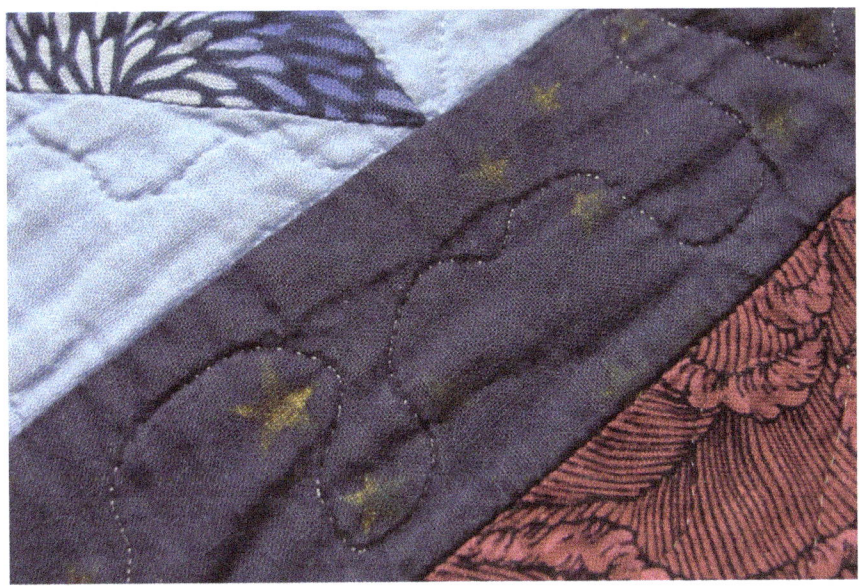

Gold print stars tarnish over time.

Some fabric problems take a while to show up. Color fastness, the stability of the dye, is apparent only when the quilt gets wet. I had a woman call about washing an antique red and white quilt. It was in a flood and she found it afterwards a block away from her house. She was worried about washing it, wondering how to test if the red dye would bleed. And then we both slapped our foreheads—the quilt had been wet for days before she found it and nothing bled.

On the other hand, I bought yards of a gray fabric with little blue flowers and when I prewashed it, the little flowers streaked to new positions.

I don't always prewash my new fabrics, but I do test them before putting them into a quilt. See testing instructions in Chapter 2.

Another issue is light fastness. The industry standard for quilting cottons is 20 hours of light exposure without fading. Many fabrics do much better than that.

However, in a wall hanging in which I had two different navy blue fabrics, it was disconcerting to see one turn lavender. There again, testing could have helped me (Chapter 2).

In 1969 I was forced to take Home Economics. My mother had already taught me to sew clothing, but the Home Ec teacher taught us to straighten fabric. The idea was that fabric on the bolt may have stretched and the warp and weft might not be perfectly perpendicular to each other. We could stretch it back into place.

Don't bother trying to do this with quilting cottons. Likely the cut ends of your yardage will not be perpendicular to the selvedge edges. That's fine. However, the cross grain of the weave of the fabric should be perpendicular, 90 degrees, to the selvedges.

Hold the yardage in front of you, cut edges at top and bottom (or torn edges to find the cross grain), folding in half, fold in one hand and selvage edges in the other. Get the selvedge edges parallel to each other, and to the fold, for the length of the fabric. I put one index finger into the top of the fold and the other between the two selvedge corners and then adjust the corners up and down until the selvedge edges hang parallel.

If you are tempted to stretch the fabric to make it behave, don't. It has a manufacturing defect. Relegate this piece to the animal shelter for making pillows for homeless cats.

Unless you truly need to make a quick, disposable quilt, use the best fabric available. You and your quilt deserve it.

Other Materials

Quilt longevity depends on more than quality fabric. I found out the hard way that thread and fabric should be compatible. Years ago, I pieced cotton and polyester fabrics with polyester thread to make a quilted couch pillow. The pillow got a lot of hard use. The polyester thread, much stronger than the cotton fabric, sawed right through it along the seam line. With the seam allowance cut off, there was no way to repair the patchwork. However, the polyester fabric was fine. That was 1983. I no longer make quilts with polyester fabrics or piece them with polyester thread.

Strong polyester thread sawed through the weak cotton fabric, but not the stronger, narrow border of polyester fabric.

A few years later, I brought home two tied patchwork quilts my mother made for my sister and me when we were little. All the diagonal seams popped open because the cotton thread used for piecing broke. I could re-stitch the seams because the seam allowances were still intact. Then I added a lot more yarn ties so that the quilt tops had more support from the backings and the diagonal seams wouldn't be under so much stress.

When I started quilting in 1978 everything was tied or quilted by hand. We were always trying to get away with the least amount of quilting so we could move on to new projects. Remembering my mom's quilts, I told students to always use cotton thread for piecing cotton fabrics. Now with the advent of copious machine quilting, there is very little chance that patchwork seams will ever flex enough to come undone. If your quilting lines are less than an inch apart, it might not matter if your thread and fabric are not of the same substance, or the piecing thread is stronger than the fabric.

I do have reservations about using "plastic" in quilts. Polyester and all its cousins are everywhere in quilting: thread, trims, batting. The woman who taught me to hand quilt in 1983 made lots of polyester double-knit quilts because everyone kept giving her fabric they found to be uncomfortable to wear—it didn't breathe. We joked that her quilts would never disintegrate and in the distant future, archeologists will find only her quilts.

I'm not so sure now that plastic materials will age that well. Some get brittle. Some turn yellow. Some get sticky. And that's before being subjected to attic temperatures. I already know that polyester batting in a quilt used nightly for 10 years completely loses its loft. And I'm not sure the pilling problem—little polyester batting fibers poking through to the quilt surface and then tying themselves together in knotty pills—has been solved. However, once again, copious machine quilting might keep the batting from rubbing against the fabrics and poking through as much.

The biggest reason for using natural fibers for quilt batting—silk, wool and cotton (I don't count bamboo because it is more like polyester after all the processing) is breathability. Polyester may feel warmer, but natural fiber bed linens are more comfortable with a wider range of temperatures. Comfort may be a deciding factor in whether a quilt is reserved for beds rather than the trunk of the car for emergencies or picnics.

I'm also concerned about quilt-making aids that add chemicals to your quilt that are not washed out when the quilt is finished. Fusibles come to mind. I think they are great fun for wall hangings. Fabric paints and markers fall in the same category, as do most non-fabric embellishments. There's just no telling yet how some of these things will age.

We don't know how the chemicals in plastic buttons and the finish on wooden dinosaurs will interact with fabric over time.

I once saw some of Grandma Moses's original artwork when it was on exhibit in Washington, D.C. She had decided to embellish her snow scenes with salt to make them sparkle. Except over the years all the added "snow" turned black. Or maybe it was the glue.

Don't hesitate to experiment with all the latest quilt-making aids and materials. But when it comes to your heirloom-worthy quilt, ask yourself, "What did Great-Grandma do? How do her quilts look 100 years later?"

After 22 years, my Kool-Aid dyed fabrics (the plain fabrics) have turned brown in some places (upper center). The commercial print fabric, overdyed in several colors by a studio using fabric dye, is fine.

Quilt-making Techniques

Great-Grandma's longest-lived quilts have a couple of construction methods in common. In addition to lots of quilting that covers every patch, as mentioned previously, they have double binding protecting the edges. If a quilt is finished by bringing the backing over the edge, or the border of the top of the quilt to the back, and the edge begins to wear, you can add double binding made from an appropriate fabric. See a quilt-making instruction book or go online for directions.

Chapter 2 – Test

A smudge of dye migrated from the dark fabric into the light fabric.

In the last chapter, I listed choices you can make that will prolong a quilt's life before you even begin sewing. There is another: testing.

Will fabric dyes bleed and make your quilt unattractive? You can throw your new yardage in the washer and dryer and that will take care of a lot of excess dye problems. Or, like Harriet Hargrave, author of "From Fiber to Fabric," you can test a swatch.

If you see dye bleeding out of the swatch, it doesn't tell you if it will wash away or re-attach itself to some other fabric in your quilt.

If you air-dry your quilt instead of using the clothes dryer, it might take long enough that the rogue dyes will have a chance to migrate along seam lines to a lighter fabric, or along quilting lines to the other side of the quilt.

Testing under extreme conditions will tell you what happens if the quilt is washed "the wrong way."

Testing for Bleeding

When preparing to make a major quilt, I make a quiltlet, piecing 2-inch squares of all the fabrics, alternating darks and lights in a checkerboard. In the case of a Double Wedding Ring quilt, I made one of the arcs to practice the curved piecing technique.

I layer the little piece of patchwork with the batting and backing I intend to use and quilt it, making sure I stitch through each fabric.

Then I put it in a bowl of boiling water with a little bit of regular or extra-strength laundry soap or detergent and let it soak about 30 minutes before laying it out on a towel to dry—mimicking all the worst-case scenarios that might promote bleeding and staining if an uninformed launderer washes the quilt.

When the quiltlet is dry, I check the light-colored fabrics adjacent to dark fabrics for any bleeding. Then I check along the quilting lines on the front and back for any other bleeding. In the case of one quilt that was going to be made of hand-dyed fabrics, the white backing of the quiltlet became stained with pink from a hot pink patch on the front.

Testing fabrics this way may also tell you if one is substandard for other reasons, such as excessive shrinkage or fading.

The test quiltlet on the left shows no bleeding, just fraying of the backing along the edge. However, on the quiltlet on the right, shown back side up, color from the hand-dyed fabric on the front bled onto the white backing along the right edge.

If, after washing your quiltlet (or your quilt if you didn't take time to test fabrics—but don't boil it!), dye has migrated, quickly treat spots with a commercial stain remover and put the quilt back in the wash. You might also want to throw in a handful of Shout Color Catcher sheets. And after this treatment, you'll want to dry the quilt quickly so dye has no time to migrate again. If a color catcher-type product is not available, be prepared to treat stains if any dyes bleed.

Testing for Light-fastness

Light-fastness is something else you can test if you aren't in a big hurry to start your project.

Cut a 2-inch square of each fabric and tape them to a sunny, south-facing window for a couple of weeks, then compare with the original yardage. Navy blue is the unstable color I've seen most often, turning lavender.

I didn't test for light-fastness back in 1995 and now I have a wall hanging with a block that's lavender and pink instead of navy blue and pink. In another block in the same quilt, a different navy blue fabric, which has had the same exposure to light, is still strong.

Both the dot print on the left and the dot print on the right started out with navy blue backgrounds. Though receiving the same amount of light, one faded more.

Chapter 3 – Use

Protect the edge of the quilt by turning the top sheet back over it.

A bed is a safe place for a quilt to lie. No stress on seams, dim light, and temperatures comfortable for humans and textiles.

The lucky quilt is protected from jumping pets, stuff thrown on it and people sitting on it. But it's hard to train family members to flip back the quilt before sitting down or packing a suitcase on the bed.

Simple bedmaking can be hard on a quilt too if someone grabs the top edge and just pulls. It is better to lift the quilt into place instead of tugging. Quilts slept under always seem to migrate to the foot of the bed. If you are sleeping under two or three quilts, every few mornings you must peel back to the first layer, straighten that one out and then replace the others one at a time.

The top edge of a quilt also gets a lot of wear from the oils from our hands and faces, and the roughness of men's beards. I like to make square quilts so the edges can be rotated and take turns being the top edge—then they all get equal wear. The best protection is a generous amount of sheet turned over the quilt's edge.

Long ago, housewives basted fabric "beard guards" over the top edge of a quilt. These wrapped over the edge, extending maybe 10 inches on both front and back. Quilt appraiser and historian Jeananne Wright told me they were loosely sewn or basted on and the industrious housewives took them off on a regular basis for washing.

Protecting a quilt from body oils and dirt means having to wash it less often. The less you wash a quilt, the less wear and tear. On the other hand, body oils and dirt left on a quilt will age the fabric. Body oils become stains. And dirt, even dust, has sharp edges that fray fabric fibers over time.

Conservation of your quilt must be balanced with use and enjoyment. Some quilts are destined to be dragged by small children or spilled on while eating in front of the TV. Hopefully, those aren't the ones you put too much time into making.

If your quilt wears out prematurely from love and normal but hard use, take that as a compliment.

The edge of this 1920s-era quilt is stained and shattered by hard use.

Jeananne Wright shares this example of a beard guard. This one is made with a geometric patchwork print known as "cheater cloth" because it looks like pieced patchwork but isn't. Wrapped around the edge of a quilt and basted in place, it protects the top edge of the quilt from men's rough beards and the oils from hands and faces. Photo copyrighted by Jeananne Wright.

Chapter 4 – Display

The surface of the wooden quilt display rod is sealed to prevent it from interacting with the fabric.

Spreading your quilts on beds is only one way to display them. Many of us drape quilts over other furniture (avoiding unsealed wood), fold and stack them on open shelves or hang them on the wall.

Quilts on display don't get the same rough physical treatment as quilts used for warmth. Instead, light is the biggest problem. If you've replaced your windows with energy efficient, "low e" (low-emissivity) glass, you may have somewhat reduced the fading problem caused by the ultraviolet wavelength in sunlight. Jeananne Wright has had her windows coated with a UV-resistant film to protect her quilt collection.

Artificial lighting also has UV rays. Fluorescent lighting is the worst. Look for products that can filter UV from light bulbs.

It is inevitable that quilts will fade if they spend any time with enough light to be seen, so consider keeping them in the dark when you aren't looking at them.

At least make sure your quilt fades evenly. A quilt faded along an exposed fold looks worse than a quilt with overall fading. Refold quilts on display often. For those decorating the back of the couch, flip the quilt around often so the same corner isn't illuminated by the same sunbeam each day.

One recommendation, from http://www.museumtextiles.com/, is to rotate quilts on display every 6 months. In a bright location, I think you should rotate them even more often. This is the justification you need to make or collect lots of quilts—at least one for each season for each display location!

After light, dirt is the other issue for quilts on display: dust, pollution, household cleaning product fumes, pet hair, wood smoke, tobacco smoke, greasy cooking vapors. You may want to wash a quilt that has been on display before rotating it into storage.

Over the last 30 years the quilting community has developed a nearly standardized tube-type sleeve for hanging quilts, protecting the quilt from the rod, and with less distortion. Never tack a quilt to the wall or a frame.

Use your imagination for ways to support the ends of the rod when hanging it. A rod can be cut almost the width of the quilt to hide it, or a little longer, for insertion into decorative brackets.

If your quilt design can also be enjoyed hung from the opposite edge of the quilt, you can add a second sleeve and trade off which way you hang it. For art quilts that need a little help hanging absolutely straight, slide another rod in the second sleeve on the lower edge.

Keep in mind that the fibers of a hanging quilt, especially a large quilt, can stretch and that every three months or so it is good to let them relax while you hang a different quilt.

How to Make a Hanging Sleeve

Perhaps using leftover fabric from the back of the quilt, piece a strip of fabric 9 inches wide and the same length as the width of the quilt. If it is for a king-sized quilt, cut the length in half to make two sleeves, allowing for a middle rod support.

Hem the short edges of the strip by turning under ½ inch towards the right side (or the wrong side if you prefer) of the strip, pressing, and turning under again. For a hand-quilted quilt, consider hand-stitching this hem in place as if you were hemming a skirt, slipping the needle inside the fold and then out for a tiny, nearly invisible stitch into the tube before slipping the needle back inside the fold. For a machine-quilted quilt, topstitch the hem in place.

Match the two long edges with wrong sides together and stitch using a ½-inch seam allowance. Wrong sides together mean you won't need to turn the tube right side out. The seam allowances will be hidden between the tube and the quilt.

Press this seam open while pressing the tube flat. At the same time, center the seam on the side of the tube facing up. Be careful the seam doesn't get wavy or begin to spiral. Keep it centered.

Then flip the tube over, putting the seam against the ironing board. Use a ruler to help you to fold up one long edge of the tube exactly 1 inch (both layers), and press the fold in place. Now your tube has four parallel, pressed edges (open the tube a little to see the inverted fourth one). You will be stitching the tube to the quilt along the two pressed folds closest to the lengthwise seam. Ignore the other folds. Measure the distance between the two folds you will be stitching along.

On the quilt, mark a line across the back 1 to 2 inches below the top edge of the quilt, and another line below, parallel to the first line, at the distance you measured.

Center the sleeve, matching the two folds to the two lines and pin in place. If you used pencil to mark the lines, make sure the sleeve overlaps just enough that the lines don't show. If you used a washout marker, it isn't necessary to hide the lines if you will be washing the quilt soon.

Use either a whip stitch or a large version of your favorite applique stitch to sew along the pinned folds, catching generous amounts of the quilt backing and batting. Jeananne Wright recommends taking a stitch all the way through the front of the quilt every 6 inches to relieve the pull on the batting and backing. Also, sew down the short ends of the sleeve that are against the back of the quilt. That will keep hanging rods from accidentally being inserted between the quilt and the sleeve.

The quilt sleeve pouches to accommodate the shape of the display rod so that the front of the quilt will hang flat. This quilt's hanging sleeve was made from three strips of leftover fabric pieced together: two strips of plain yellow and one strip floral. The hem at the end of the sleeve has been turned to the wrong side.

Chapter 5 – Air

A couple of clean, damp dishtowels in the dryer on air or very low heat with your quilt will freshen it and remove animal hair.

For many, quilt care directions seem to be synonymous with quilt washing instructions. Just when does a quilt need washing? When it has actual dirt on it, or actual body oils.

Quilts can often smell musty after being in storage, but that doesn't mean they need washing. Each washing shortens the lifespan of a quilt. On the other hand, grit can cause fabric wear.

Sometimes, all a quilt needs is a good airing. If it has been folded up, lay it out on a bed. Maybe open a window to get some cross ventilation.

If it is too smelly for indoor airing, go outside. Find a shady place to lay a sheet on the lawn, with the quilt on top, and another sheet over it—to protect it from the birds and sun. This is supposing you have a nice lawn and the wind isn't blowing. Here in Wyoming most days the quilt would soon be in the neighbor's yard or in Nebraska.

Resist the temptation to put your quilt on the clothesline—it's hard on the stitching, although today's densely machine-quilted quilts are probably up to the task if they are in good repair—but only if they are dry. I have multiple parallel clotheslines I can lay a quilt over—though I need to clean the plastic-coated lines first or put a sheet over them. Using a protective sheet on top is a good idea in this instance, too.

Dryer

Company is coming and you don't have time to lay the extra quilts outside for the day. Instead, try this if the quilt is colorfast: Wet two or three colorfast hand towels and throw them and the quilt in the dryer on a low heat setting, or even just on air, for 10-15 minutes. If the quilt gets too damp, remove the towels.

This moist, low heat in the dryer also helps take out fold lines and removes pet hair.

Vacuum

Fragile antiques and wall hangings, especially those with painted surfaces or 3-D embellishments, need to be treated as art works. Professional conservators vacuum art quilts with a hose attachment with a brush end, but the quilts need to be protected from being sucked up. Use a new, clean piece of fiberglass window screen with all the edges taped and lay it on the section of the quilt being vacuumed.

Chapter 6 – Wash

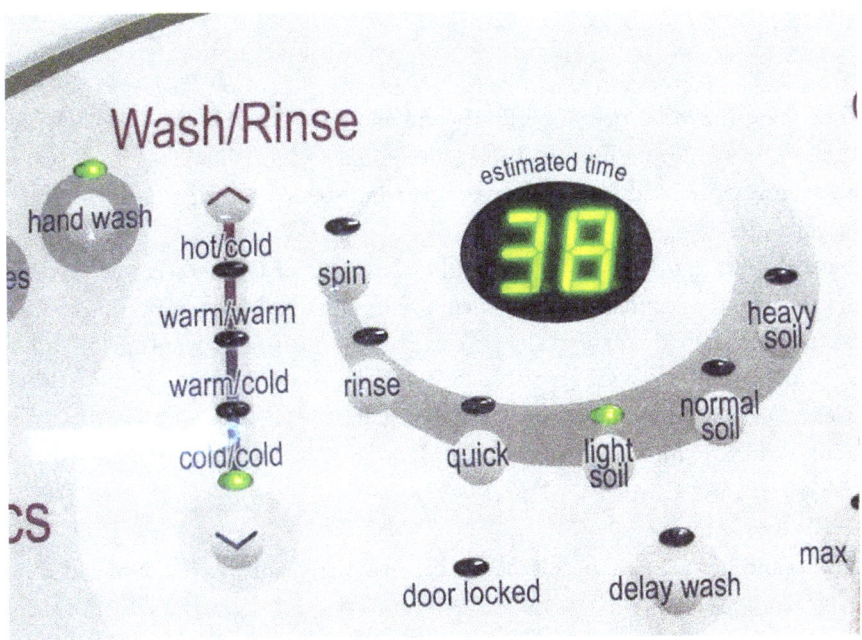

A strong quilt will do well in a top loading machine if the agitation cycles are skipped, or in a front loading washing machine set for "hand wash."

You've done your best to keep your quilt dirt-free (Chapter 3) and you've aired it regularly to keep it smelling nice (Chapter 5), but now you think it needs to be washed. It is best to avoid washing quilts, but if you, the quilt owner, feel it is necessary, here is information to help you avoid common pitfalls such as colors bleeding and stitches breaking.

If you made the quilt, you already tested the fabrics for washability (Chapter 2). If you didn't make the quilt, and it has never been washed before, do a test for bleeding on these kinds of fabrics: color saturated, especially red and dark blue; and any hand-dyed.

Test for Color Stability

Wet a piece of white cotton fabric or a cotton Q-tip and rub it on the potential bleeder to see if the dye transfers. It doesn't necessarily mean this excess dye will transfer to the rest of the quilt, but if color rubs off, you'll want to treat the quilt as if it would.

If you might have bleeding problems, get a box of Shout Color Catcher sheets and use multiple sheets per quilt per wash. Again, if a color catcher-type product is not available, be prepared to treat stains if the dye bleeds.

If the quilt is well-used, be sure to inspect it for any damage and sew up any tears and patch any holes. If this is a valuable antique quilt, let the experts repair the quilt (or instruct you on how to do it). However, the washing directions here are not for antique or fragile quilts.

Soap

The soap should be free of perfumes and additives. Harriet Hargrave, who tested soaps for her book, "From Fiber to Fabric," recommends Ivory liquid or Orvus. Orvus is readily found at quilt and fabric shops repacked in 8-ounce jars, or at feed stores in 7.5-pound containers.

Several years ago, when Mark Lipinski was editor of Quilter's Home, his readers around the country conducted a test of laundry detergents to see which protected fabric color the best. Identical sample quilts were washed 20 times each. Here are the results:

Best: Soak
Good: Dreft, Synthrapol, Miracle II Laundry Ball
Fair: Arm & Hammer, Woolite, Tide, Gain
Marginal: Surf, Cheer, MelaPower
A Washout: Amway

Orvus and Ivory liquid, both soaps rather than detergents, were not included in the test. Orvus soap is a bit odd. It is a white solid at 65 degrees. Even if it's warm enough to be a liquid, mix it with half a cup of warm water before pouring it into the soap dispenser. A tablespoon or less of the paste is enough for a queen-sized quilt. Use even less for smaller quilts. Too much soap and you will be rinsing forever, though Orvus and Ivory rinse out better than most.

What you won't need are bleach, fabric softener and any other laundry aids—unless the quilt has a stain. Then try one of the spray-on stain removers to treat spots.

Front Loading Machine

Find a front loading washing machine. Avoid a commercial machine used for washing oily clothes or that has soap residue (run it empty to see if suds develop). Chlorine-free water would be nice. A nearby dryer capable of very low heat settings may be useful.

Set front loading machines for cold wash, cold rinse, and the hand wash cycle—or the lowest amount of "agitation" possible. Add an extra rinse or plan to send the quilt through a complete cycle again without soap. The "Max Extract" spin setting is good. The more water extracted from your quilt at the end, the better.

Top Loading Machine

For top loaders, fill with cool water. Mix in the soap. Turn the machine off and add the quilt. Use your hands instead of the agitation cycle for a few minutes, gently lifting and moving the quilt. Then let the quilt soak 10 minutes before setting the washer controls for the rinse cycle. Substitute your hands again for the agitation in the rinse cycle, then let it spin. If in doubt as to whether all the soap is out, run it through another washing again, without soap.

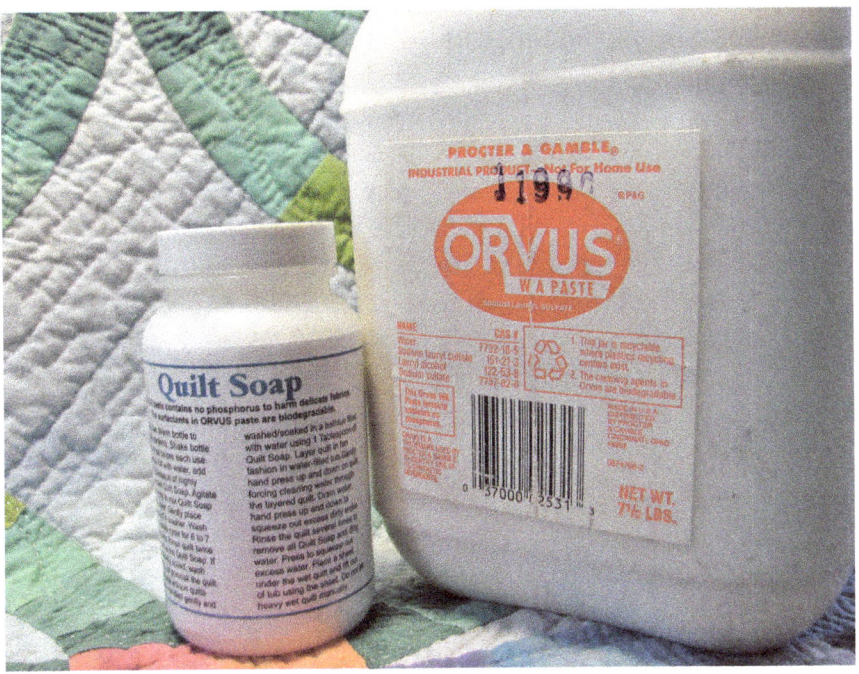

At quilt shops, you will find Orvus soap in 8-ounce jars repackaged by Quilter's Rule and labeled as "Quilt Soap." At feed stores it comes in 7.5-pound containers. This simple soap is easier on quilts than detergents with brighteners and other ingredients.

Before Drying

With either machine, top loader or front loader, when finished, check immediately to see if there was any bleeding. Never let a quilt sit in a wet lump. You might find that otherwise well-behaved colors start running around.

If there is any bleeding, treat with stain remover and rewash the quilt immediately with Color Catcher sheets, then recheck immediately—and plan to dry that quilt fairly quickly in the dryer.

Bathtub Method

Other quilt care information sources will describe how to wash a quilt in the bathtub. You lay a sheet in the bottom of the tub. Then you add the water, soap and quilt (sort of accordion-folded to fit). Let it soak 10 minutes before gently agitating the quilt by hand and then draining the tub.

Next you do several rounds of rinsing: refilling the tub, agitating the quilt, and draining the tub, all the while on your knees while bent over the edge of the tub. Finally, you press as much water out of the quilt (do not wring it) as you can. In the end, you have a heavy, wet quilt—and an aching back. The sheet helps you lift the quilt out so there is less strain on the stitching.

Then you must carefully lay your quilt out to dry on top of a clean sheet spread over a clean, colorfast surface. Because the quilt will be much wetter than one that went through the washer's spin cycle, you may want to completely cover the quilt with color-fast bath towels. Gently roll up the quilt, with the towels, then unroll it and remove the towels. Throw the towels in the dryer. When they are dry, lay them out on the quilt again and roll again. Once some of the moisture is removed this way, it may be easier to block, or square up, the quilt.

Unless you need to examine areas of the quilt during the process of washing, the washing machine (minus the top loader's agitation cycle) is safer. If you think your quilt is too fragile for the machine, it may be too fragile to be washed at all.

Dry Cleaning

Dry cleaning is not recommended for quilts.

Chapter 7 – Dry

The best way to dry a quilt is flat on the floor.

    A wet quilt is a delicate thing. The larger it is, the heavier it is and the more carefully it must be treated to make sure the weight doesn't break stitches. However, a heavily machine-quilted quilt is probably stronger than one with widely-spaced machine or hand stitching.

    It's best to air dry quilts flat. I lay a clean sheet over polyester or nylon carpet and then spread the quilt, squaring it up, blocking it. You could instead protect the floor with clean plastic sheeting and then put a layer of towels on top of it before laying out the quilt. Jeananne Wright dries quilts front side down first so that any remaining dirt will wick to the top—the back of the quilt. This is more of an issue with bathtub-washed quilts.

    Here in Wyoming, even quilts with cotton batting are dry in a few hours. Quilts with wool and polyester batting dry faster. If necessary, set up a fan to speed the drying process.

    If I use the "max extract" option on my washing machine, the quilt is so compressed by the end of the washing that I opt to toss it in the dryer on very low heat or just air for 10 minutes to loosen it up and get rid of the wrinkles, making it easier to spread. Some quilters, before the quilt on the floor is completely dry, will pick it up and pop it in the dryer to fluff it on air, no heat.

If you think any of the fabrics might bleed (you didn't make the quilt or you didn't take steps in Chapter 2 to check fabric washability), forget air drying—put the quilt in the dryer immediately, before the dyes have a chance to migrate. Use a low heat setting.

One reason we avoid using the dryer is to lessen wear and tear on the quilt. It's up to you to decide between air drying or machine drying. Weigh the potential for color migration as the quilt dries slowly, versus the surfaces of the quilt rubbing against each other in mild abrasion. I think a stain from a bleeding fabric might be worse.

Line drying kills quilts, especially if the quilt is large and clothes-pinned. Stitching will break. However, a small, hard-used crib quilt will probably be just fine over a line.

For other utility quilts, if you have multiple parallel clotheslines—my 1960s-era setup has four—you can spread a quilt out over the top of all of them. Any ridges you get from the clotheslines should disappear as the quilt is used. Be sure to wash the clotheslines or cover them with a sheet first. And put a sheet over the quilt to protect it from passing birds and the sun.

Chapter 8 – Store

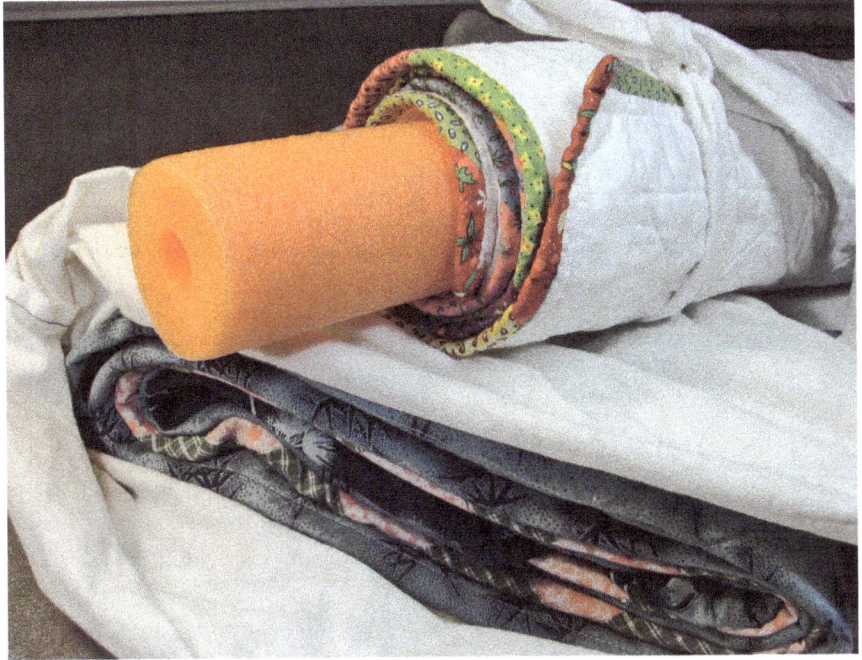

If you can't store quilts flat, rolled or carefully folded may work for you.

The best way to store a quilt is flat, in the dark, protected from dirt and interactions with chemicals, and at a temperature and level of humidity people find comfortable. The ideal temperature for textiles is 65 to 75 degrees Fahrenheit and with relative humidity at 50 percent. Layering a few quilts on your guest bed comes close, especially if you layer clean old sheets between them.

However, most of us must make a compromise with textile collection standards. I fold my big quilts, but I try to fold them in unprecise thirds or on the bias, and differently each time. I don't want to end up with that permanent crease down the middle that is seen in so many antique quilts. After folding a quilt in thirds lengthwise (or widthwise for a change), I then loosely roll, rather than fold, big quilts in the opposite direction. This makes a burrito-like shape that fits in extra-long pillow cases I make for each quilt, either out of cheap, washed muslin or the quilt's fabric leftovers.

I roll small quilts, but not tightly. I use a swim noodle or other cylinder covered in batting and muslin scraps that is a bit longer than the quilt is wide. I roll the quilt around it, not tightly, tying it loosely with a couple leftover fabric strips. I often roll more than one quilt on a noodle and top it all off with a covering of muslin. In my closet, I stand the rolled quilts upright on the protruding ends of the cylinders.

The National Park Service Museum Handbook suggests rolling quilts face out with the backside of the quilt against the tube. That way the lining of the quilt gets the wrinkles, not the front of the quilt. A quilted wall hanging should be rolled horizontally so that weight of the hanging quilt will help it uncurl.

I place fragile quilts in acid-free cardboard boxes. First, I line the boxes with washed muslin. Then I crumple pieces of muslin instead of tissue paper and stuff them in the quilt folds so they won't get compressed. Jeananne Wright uses quilt batting to stuff the folds.

At least once or twice a year it is good to unpack stored quilts, unfold them, inspect them for damage from pests or moisture, wash their fabric wrappings, and enjoy them.

Avoid

Raw wood shelves or cedar chest interiors. Raw wood in contact with fabric will stain fabric over time. Wrap the quilt in muslin or line the shelves and cedar chest in Tyvek, an inert material. Tyvek is used to wrap houses as part of the construction process. It is available in 3-foot wide rolls of 100 to 150 feet long. You may find smaller rolls (without the brand name printing all over them) through companies providing museum conservation supplies.

Plastic, especially any not of archival quality. Plastic gives off gases. There are different kinds of plastic and some are considered safe. Safe plastics are #2 HDPE, High Density Polyethylene (what milk jugs are made with) and #5 PP, Polypropylene (like yogurt containers).

While a plastic tub might do an excellent job of protecting a quilt from dirt, smells and insects, if there was any dampness when the quilt was put in the tub, mildew will grow. Be sure to add a desiccant to absorb moisture, like those little pillows included in shoe boxes (see Resources list of archival supply companies), but don't let it come in direct contact with the quilt. Although bags made of Tyvek are being promoted for quilt storage, I'd be concerned about trapping moisture in them.

Dirty, smelly or smoky places. Dust or dirt can wear out cotton fibers. Quilts absorb smells and those smells are the result of chemicals that may also damage fibers. The less you need to wash the quilt, the longer it will last.

Extreme temperatures, especially fluctuations. Attic heat dries out fibers and makes them brittle. Constant cold is not so much a problem, but not advisable.

Water pipes. Although modern basements are often finished and quite livable, know where the water pipes are and avoid leaving quilts (and other important belongings) under them.

Huge stack. Don't stack quilts more than three deep or the lower ones will get compressed. Stacking folded quilts will leave fold lines, even more of a problem.

Mothballs. Mothballs in concentrations high enough to be effective can be dangerous to anyone exposed to them, not just the pests. Instead, make sure items are clean before storing them in a container or bag.

If you think a quilt could be infested with moth larvae and eggs, freeze it, as Jeananne Wright does. Washing it in hot water might work too, but it is hard on the quilt. Less harmful is wrapping the quilt in plastic and freezing it for a few days. Remove any dead bodies, refreeze and remove any other bodies afterwards. Make sure the closet or storage area is clean before putting the quilt back.

Some websites mention lavender or other herbs as alternative moth preventatives, and others say they are not effective. Make sure to protect your quilt from direct contact with any substances.

Avoid stacking quilts for long-term storage. Otherwise, stack quilts no more than three high. Refold and rearrange frequently so the same quilt is not crushed on the bottom or the same folds exposed to light. The quilts should not be in contact with raw wood.

Chapter 9 – Appraise

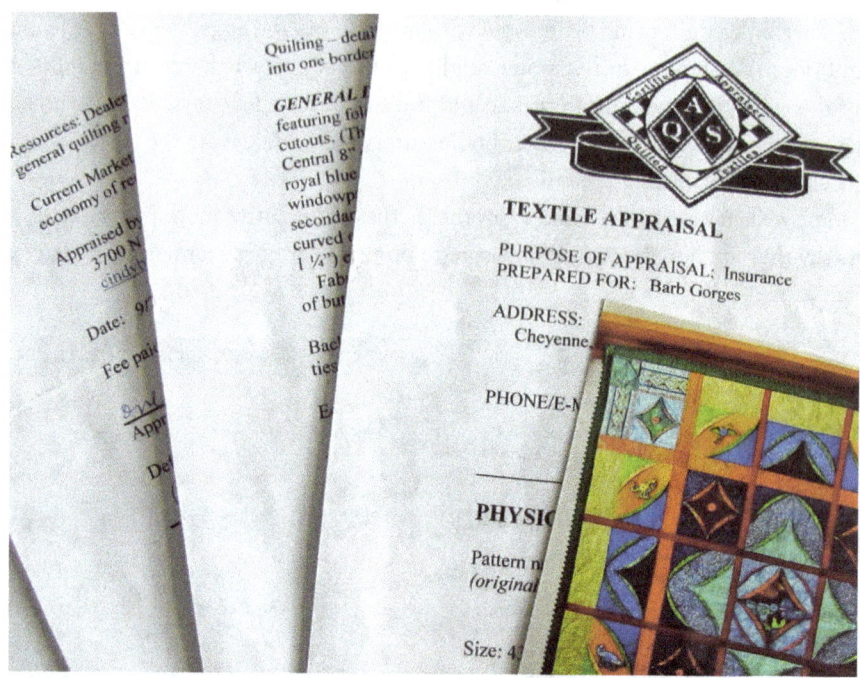

An American Quilter's Society certified appraisal can document the value of a quilt for insurance purposes.

Have your important quilts professionally appraised. Attaching value to a quilt may help keep it in better condition over the years. After all, if the next owner of the quilt has a copy of the appraisal, they might decide their dog will enjoy sleeping on a $30 store-bought comforter just as much as a handmade quilt valued at $1000.

There are three different kinds of appraisals. Fair market and donation appraisals are based on market value, what the quilt would sell for between a knowledgeable and willing seller and a knowledgeable buyer. The third, the insurance appraisal, gives you the replacement value, the value we give to our home owner's insurance company or when shipping the quilt.

If the quilt's pattern is popular, made from a well-known quilter's book or kit, replacement might be as simple as finding one for sale. In that case, replacement value would be close to market value. Otherwise, replacement value is the cost of remaking the quilt, both materials and labor. A quilt made by a prize-winning quilter will be valued higher because a quilter with equivalent workmanship skills would need to be hired and that costs more.

The American Quilter's Society's certified quilt appraisers have the best credibility. If there are none in your state, check surrounding states. You may be able to make an appointment with a quilt appraiser at a quilting event. See the Resources section for more information about the American Quilter's Society's certified appraiser program.

If you have multiple quilts you'd like to have appraised at one time, ask the appraiser if they can offer you a better deal.

You could have several of your quilts appraised to document the value of your quilt-making skill level. Then inventory all the quilts you have. If you need to make an insurance claim for a quilt you made that hasn't been appraised, you might be able to compare it to one that has been appraised. Document size, pattern, fabrics, techniques, and take photos of the whole quilt as well as its details.

I document all the quilts I make as I finish them, including a brief statement about the inspiration or occasion for which they were made and who received them—much like my quilt labels. For each one I like to include snippets of all the fabrics used and a list of where the quilt has been exhibited. Each quilt gets a page in an archival plastic sleeve in a binder—a quilt version of scrapbooking.

Scan your quilt records and appraisals if they aren't already in digital format and store them in a digital cloud. Store a hard copy at home and the original in your safe deposit box. Otherwise, appraisals won't do you any good if your house succumbs to a natural disaster.

Chapter 10 – Insure

Documenting your quilts will help with insurance claims—and provide memories of quilts you've given away.

We quilters tend to undervalue the quilts we've made. If you purchase something for your home that costs $500 or as much as several thousand dollars, wouldn't you want your homeowner's insurance to cover it if it were lost due to theft, fire or flood?

In addition to quilters undervaluing hand-made quilts, homeowner's insurance companies do as well. Without a written appraisal, they equate them to a purchased bedspread.

To get more appropriate coverage, you must have your quilts appraised (as we discussed in the last chapter), or at least have several of the important ones you've made appraised to get a sense of the expertise and value of your work. If you purchased an antique quilt, the bill of sale will help value it, but family antique quilts will need to be appraised.

No insurance company is going to pay a claim for replacement value without proof. At the most, they might pay for materials and not the labor of making the quilt. Follow the suggestions in Chapter 9 for documentation and appraisals.

Contact your insurance company to see if they will cover your quilts, perhaps with a rider, as they would art or jewelry. If they will, be sure you get the terms in writing.

If you will have your quilt on exhibit at a quilt show, find out if the quilt show is providing insurance coverage.

Maria Elkins experienced losing a quilt (and getting it back), which led her to set up the website, lostquilt.com, where information and photos for missing quilts can be posted—and perhaps recognized. She also has more detailed information about insuring quilts.

A baby quilt I made was lost in transit for seven weeks between Wyoming and New Jersey. The quilt was not appraised so quite likely the insurance offered through the shipper would have only paid the cost of materials to make it. I had receipts for the recently purchased fabric for the backing and binding and my usual page of documentation including fabric samples and photo. Looking later at an appraisal of a similarly sized quilt I made, I should have increased the amount for which I insured it.

Consider signing your quilt somewhere obscure, like under the binding before sewing it in place. Then you can uncover it if the quilt's provenance is ever in dispute.

Insurance always seems expensive, but it is a small price in comparison to losing a quilt.

Chapter 11 – Ship

The quilt to be shipped should fit the box perfectly. Empty box corners get crushed and torn. This quilt has been folded like an accordion, map, or fan in both directions, distributing bulky folds evenly.

In the previous two chapters, I discussed appraising a quilt and insuring it. It is important to take care of these two items before shipping an important quilt. If the quilt is valued for more than the maximum the shipping company can insure, make up the difference with a temporary insurance policy, especially if the quilt is going to a show.

When shipping to a quilt show, be sure to exactly follow the show's directions. The major shows have instructions that help them receive and track quilt entries and return them.

Make sure the mailing label is securely fastened to the box. Make sure it doesn't say "quilt" anywhere (if mailing to say, the Pieceable Quilters Guild, use their initials instead, or maybe the name of someone on the show committee). Make sure your name, address and phone number are on a card securely pinned to the quilt. And it is not paranoid to write your name, address and phone number on the quilt's documentation label. It makes it easier for quilt show volunteers to double-check they have the right quilt going to the right place at the end of the show.

If you are shipping a quilt as a gift to someone, don't surprise them. Double check their address. Find out which carrier they trust the most. Find out if they will be home when you plan to ship the quilt.

Find out if it would be best to ship the quilt to your recipient's work place instead or some other location where they trust someone to receive it. You can pay extra for a signature to be required when the package is delivered. In some locations, the recipient can arrange to pick up a package from a UPS location rather than have UPS leave it on their doorstep.

Once you ship the quilt, send the recipient the online tracking information, though if anything goes wrong, you will still be the only one allowed to make inquiries. If you used a shipping service like The UPS Store, they are the shipper and they make the inquiries.

If your quilt is small enough, avoid creases by wrapping it around a swim noodle or cardboard roll and ship it in a tube or long box.

If folding the quilt, fold it like a map or fan, wide enough to fit the box one way and then fold it to fit the other dimension of the box the same way in the other direction. This distributes bulky folds more evenly. Pin a copy of the mailing label to the quilt. Place the quilt inside a plastic bag—preferably clear so it isn't mistaken for trash. Place it in the box. A new box is safest because it is stronger than a used box. Consider double-boxing to better protect the quilt from punctures. Put an extra piece of cardboard on top of the quilt, under the box flaps, to protect it from anyone using a knife to open the box.

If there is any space left in the box, consider cutting the box down (take the quilt out while doing that) to make the quilt fit exactly or fill the empty space with Styrofoam chunks. Avoid the aggravation of Styrofoam peanuts or at least put them in plastic bags. Or use closed egg cartons. If you don't fill in its corners, the box will get crushed in transit.

Use a black marker to cover any printing on the outside of the box.

Use plenty of packing tape. Seal all the edges of the box. Put clear packing tape over the mailing label to protect it.

Once again, avoid writing the word "quilt" anywhere on the box. When filling out the shipping company's insurance form, refer to your contents as a textile, which is not as exciting to would-be thieves but still describes a quilt.

Don't wait for your quilt's new owner to send you a thankyou note. Once the tracking information shows that the quilt has been delivered, double check that it was delivered to them—and not an untrustworthy neighbor.

If your quilt is delayed by more than a few days or appears to be lost, contact the shipping company and be prepared to give them a copy of the documentation that shows the value of your quilt. For more suggestions check lostquilt.com.

Traveling

Pack your quilt in normal luggage rather than just a plastic bag, disguising it as more clothing. If you are flying with a quilt, do what you can to carry it on with you.

Photograph

Whatever you do, never let your quilt leave home without making sure you have a good photo of it. Even if you are giving it to someone as a gift, they may have occasion to ask you for a photo for their insurance agent.

Before you ship a quilt, be sure to take photos of it. This plastic sleeve with a cardstock insert includes a photo of the whole quilt and a close-up, notes about the occasion, inspiration, construction and exhibition of the quilt, and it includes the quiltlet that was made to test the fabrics for color fastness. The back of the page has several more photos.

Chapter 12 – Sign

Signature and year have been embroidered on the lower right corner of the front of three different quilts.

In the previous chapters I have touched on topics relating to quilt construction, care, and use that can help your quilt make it through several generations.

I have one final suggestion for you. Sign and date your quilt.

Recently, my cousins had to decide what to do with their now deceased parents' belongings. I'd made the parents a quilt and I told my cousins that if there were any quilts they didn't want, they could send them to me.

I am happy to report that they did keep several quilts, including the one I made, and they shipped two other quilts to me.

I was pleased to have quilts that belonged to my aunt and uncle, but neither quilt came with any information. Since neither my aunt nor uncle made quilts, I was left wondering whether an ancestor of my uncle (and mine) had made them, or perhaps someone in my aunt's family.

One quilt was obviously a Lone Star made by Native Americans and most likely presented to my aunt in the 1950s when she was a public health nurse at the Fort Berthold reservation in North Dakota.

The other is a scrap quilt with no name, no date—and it needs repairing. If my aunt's mother made it, I could save it for my cousins' children. More likely, the day my children deal with my quilt-making legacy, that quilt will end up on the discard pile, since it is one of those homely scrap quilts only a direct descendant or quilt historian could love.

Even if your quilts aren't getting passed down through your family, your name on the quilt you made will increase the likelihood that it will be taken care of.

The less anonymous the quiltmaker is, the better. The more information you provide on a label on the back, or embroider somewhere, the better. It will make it more likely your quilt will be cherished, even 100 years from now.

How to Make a Documentation Label

I use my computer to write my documentation labels. I use Arial, a sans serif font—one with no curlicues. The title size is 24 and the rest of the label is in 18 point.

I format my labels so they are rectangular, about 3 inches high by about 4 inches wide. It depends on how much information I put on one. Here's what I include:

Quilt title – Every quilt should have a name. My quilts also have numbers to help me look them up in my records.

Size – Given in inches rather than bed size.

Date – Usually the date I finished the quilt, but sometimes also the date I started the quilt.

Reason – Does this quilt celebrate a special occasion or memory?

Contents – Knowing what fibers the quilt is made of, especially the batting, which is hidden, will help anyone who washes it in the future.

Maker – Besides you, list the people who helped you. Include the quilter for hire and the pattern designer. Did friends contribute blocks? If they didn't sign them, maybe make a little chart on a bigger label to indicate who made which block.

Location – Where the quilt was made will be interesting to future quilt historians.

Owner – That's you if you aren't giving the quilt away for a few years. Include your address and phone number especially if the quilt will travel outside your home.

Copyright notice – See lostquilt.com for how original your quilt needs to be to be eligible for copyrighting.

Quilt care—A simple statement that is true for your quilt will go a long way to helping it live longer, "Wash in cool water without machine agitation, no bleach. Dry flat." Or maybe it's an art quilt: "Do Not Wash."

Documentation labels tell who made the quilt, and when, where and why it was made.

I print the label on white paper, using the "Best" printing mode so the print is good and dark.

Measuring the dimensions of the actual print area, I add a ½ inch to both height and width and then rummage through my stash for a scrap a couple inches larger.

I look for a plain fabric, or perhaps one that is mottled, avoiding prints and dark fabrics. I can usually find something from the scraps of the quilt itself. Sometimes turning over a print shows that the wrong side will work perfectly.

I cut the label fabric generously, then center it over the printout of the label and tape it in place so I can trace the lettering. Then the printout and fabric can be taped to a window, if there's daylight. If you have a clear plastic table extension for your sewing machine, you can slip a small light underneath to turn it into a light table. I use a florescent under-cabinet light.

It might be possible for your printer to print directly on fabric. But best, long-lasting results require special ink. Instead, trace your text onto the fabric with a fine-point permanent marker. Your local hobby or quilt shop should have permanent ink, textile-compatible pens.

Trim your label. I leave ½ inch all the way around and then I press ¼ inch under. I applique it to the lower left corner of the back of the quilt, right behind where my embroidered signature is on the front of the quilt.

If you want to get fancy, add a pieced border to the label. I like to do this for challenge quilts that had to include certain fabrics. Years later it helps me remember which were the challenge fabrics.

If your quilt wins any accolades, add a label that lists them. In a hundred years, the ribbons may be long gone. No one will remember your quilt was famous unless you tell them.

If you have handled any of your ancestor's belongings, you know how wonderful it is to have the story behind them, and how easy it is to forget what your mother or grandmother told you. Even if it doesn't go to family, tell your quilt's story anyway on a fabric label sewn to the quilt. Perhaps another quilter will be appreciating your work, and be inspired by it, one hundred years from now.

Acknowledgements

My first quilting mentor was Ruby McKim, through her book, "101 Patchwork Patterns," 1962 edition, which guided me in making my first quilt during a cold winter in Wisconsin, my home state.

In 1986 the Miles City Piece Makers of eastern Montana was founded and we became each other's mentors: Mugo Boe, Lorraine Butterfield, Lisa Durkee, Denise Hartse, Kookie Kwasinski, Mollie Lentz, Linda Millenbach, Edna Rovig, Laurel Shook, Daisy Sterling, Linda Schiller, Lydia Watts, Katie Wyss and many more whose names have faded from my memory.

Two-year-old Bryan and I celebrate with some of the Miles City Piece Makers in front of our house when the guild finished its second hand-quilted raffle quilt in 1987.

I found more mentoring peers with the Cheyenne Heritage Quilters, which I joined in 1989 and of which I'm still a member (and two-time quilt show chair). My quilting students at Laramie County Community College and elsewhere in Wyoming, Colorado and Nebraska have taught me about sewing and quilting as well.

Harriet Hargrave sparked my interest in quilt care issues. Her shop, "Harriet's Treadle Arts," in Wheat Ridge, Colorado, was only 100 miles away and she came several times to teach in Cheyenne. She was the first to order my Quilt Care Labels in 1998, and offer a testimonial.

Virginia Ohr, editor of the Wyoming State Quilt Guild newsletter published what amounted to rough drafts of the chapters of this book in *Patchwords*. An email from one of the members got me thinking about gathering them together.

I thank my longtime friend and fellow quilter, Florence Brown, for being the first to review the text. Also adding valuable comments were author, birder and quilter Jane L. Dorn who also provided the artwork for the Yucca Road Press logo, writer Edith Cook and grammarian Margot Joy. I am extremely grateful to Jeananne Wright, AQS appraiser, who provided technical writing expertise and used her extensive knowledge of quilting to fact check.

And lastly, for all the time he has given me to quilt, I thank my husband, Mark, who likes to cook—every day.

Resources

Books

Aug, Bobbie, Carol Butzke, Linda Hohnsberger, Gerald Roy, **"The AQS Guide to Quilt Care, 3rd Revision"** c. 2011, American Quilters Society.

Aug, Bobbie, Sharon Newman and Gerald Roy, **"Vintage Quilts: Identifying, Collecting, Dating, Preserving & Valuing"** c.2002, published by Collector Books, available through https://shop.americanquilter.com.

Gridley, Judith Scoggin, Joan Reed Kiplinger & Jessie Gridley McClure, **"Vintage Fabrics: Identification & Value Guide"** c. 2006, published by Collector Books, available through https://shop.americanquilter.com.

Hargrave, Harriet, **"From Fiber to Fabric"** c. 1997, published by C & T Publishing, http://www.ctpub.com/.

Wasserman, Ann, **"Preserving Our Quilt Legacy, Giving Antique Quilts the Special Care They Deserve, 2nd edition,"** c. 2016, published by Ann Wasserman, www.annquilts.com.

Websites

American Institute for Conservation of Historic and Artistic Works, http://www.conservation-us.org/. Topics: Caring for Your Treasures, Textiles Finding a Professional Conservator.

American Quilter's Society, P.O. Box 3290, Paducah, KY 42002-3290, http://www.americanquilter.com. Topics: Appraisers List, Appraisers Program.

AQS QuiltWeek, http://www.quiltweek.com. Topics: Hanging Sleeve Instructions.

Fairfield Processing Company, https://www.fairfieldworld.com/faq. Topics: Quilt Batting (selection and care).

Gorges Quilt Labels, https://gorgesquiltcarelabels.com/. Topics: Updates to this book.

Harriet Hargrave, http://www.harriethargrave.com. Topics: Fabric Care (laundry soaps for sale), Harriet Hargrave's Quick-Look Guide, Caring for Fabric and Quilts (card format)

Hobbs Bonded Fibers, http://www.hobbsbatting.com. Topics: Resources, For Quilters, FAQs.

Hollinger Metal Edge, 9401 Northeast Dr., Fredericksburg, VA 22408; 6340 Bandini Blvd., Commerce, CA 90040; http://www.hollingermetaledge.com. Topics: Resources, storage information, Textile storage boxes, Tyvek.

International Quilt Study Center and Museum, 1523 N. 33rd St., Lincoln, NE 68583, http://www.quiltstudy.org/. Topics: "To Protect and Preserve, Caring for Family Quilts in the Home" downloadable, free brochure.

The Kirk Collection, 1010 North 49th Ave., Omaha, NE 68132, http://kirkcollection.com. Topics: The Quilt Restoration Workshop DVD, Dating Antique Fabrics DVD.

Lost Quilt Come Home, http://lostquilt.com. Topics: Display of lost and stolen quilts, protecting quilts, displaying quilts.

Museum Textile Services, P.O. Box 5004, Andover, MA 01810; http://www.museumtextiles.com/. Topics: Textile conservation, many free resources, quilt storage and handling brochure.

National Park Service Museum Handbook Part I, https://www.nps.gov/museum/publications. Topics: Appendix K: Curatorial Care of Textile Objects.

Nebraska Extension Publications, http://extensionpubs.unl.edu. Topics: Care of Quilts (free PDF downloads).

Quilters Dream Batting, http://quiltersdreambatting.com. Topic: User Guide.

Soak Wash, http://soakwash.com. Topics: Hand or machine washing, Soak School, Quilts

Index

airing, 19
    clothesline, 20
    dryer, 10, 20
    vacuum, 20
American Quilter's Society, 31
antique quilts, 22, 27, 32
appraisal, 2, 30, 32
    appraisers, 31
    market value, 31
    replacement value, 30, 32
batting, 8, 38
beard guard, 14
bed, 13
    making, 13
bleeding, 6, 10, 26
    testing, 6, 21
body oils, 14
boxes, acid-free, 28
boxes, plastic, 28
Brown, Florence, 42
cedar chest, 2, 28
certified quilt appraiser, 31
Cheyenne Heritage Quilters, 41
clothesline, 20, 26
Color Catcher sheets, 22, 28
color fastness, 6, 21
    Kool-Aid dye, 9
    testing, 6, 21
copyright, 38
desiccant, 28
dirt, 14, 17, 19
display, 16
    hanging, 17
    rotate, 17
    sleeve, 17
documentation, 31, 37, 38
dry cleaning, 24
drying, quilt, 10, 25
    air, 10, 25
    line, 26
    machine, 26
Elkins, Maria, 33
embellishments

buttons, 9
fusibles, 8
fabric markers, 8
fabric paint, 8
fabric, 4
    batiks, 5
    color, 5
    dyes, 10
    gold highlights, 5
    finish, 6
    grain, 8
    polyester, 10
    quality, 6
    quilting cotton, 5
fading, 6, 16
folding, 27
From Fiber to Fabric, 10
fusibles, 8
Gorges Quilt Labels, 2
Grandma Moses, 8
hang tags, 2
hanging sleeve directions, 17
Hargrave, Harriet, 10, 22, 41
insurance, 30, 32
    exhibit, 33
    rider, 33
    shipping, 34
labels
    documentation, 31, 35
    mailing, 34
    making documentation, 38
    quilt care, 2, 41
lighting, 16
light fastness, 6, 12, 16
Lipinski, Mark, 22
Lostquilt.com, 33
low "e" glass, 16
McKim, Ruby, 41
Miles City Piecemakers, 41
Museumtextiles.com, 17
NPS Museum Handbook, 28
Ohr, Virginia, 42
Olsen, Anne, 2

Orvus soap, 22
paints and markers, 8
pests, 28
    moths, mothballs, 29
pets
    hair removal, 20
    on beds, 13
photographing, 31, 36
pilling, 8
plastic, 7, 28
polyester, 7
quilt
    airing, 19
    appraisal, 30
    antique, 22, 27, 32
    care information, 38
    conservation, 14
    display, 16
    drying, 25
    exhibit, 33
    folding, 27
    hanging, 17
    historians, 38
    inventory, 31
    labels, 31
    maker, 38
    making, 4
    missing, 33
    packing, 35
    records, 31
    rolling, 28
    shipping, 34
    show, 33
    signing, 2, 37
    sleeve, 17
    soap, 22
    storage, 27
    tied, 7
    use, 13
    washing, 21
quiltlet, 11, 36
Quilter's Home, 22
quiltmaker, anonymous, 38
replacement value, 30, 32
rolling, 28
shipping, 34

insurance, 34
mailing label, 34
online tracking, 35
UPS, 35
show, quilt, 33, 34
signing, 2, 37
sleeve, quilt 17
soap, 22
    Orvus, 22
    Soak, 22
    Synthrapol, 22
storage, 27
    folding, 27
    humidity, 27
    layering, 27
    moths, mothballs, 29
    rolling, 28
    stacking, 29
    temperature, 28
    Tyvek, 28
    wrapping, muslin, 28
swim noodle, 28
testing 10
    bleeding, 11
    fabric dyes, 10
    fading, 12
    light-fastness, 12
    shrinkage, 11
thread, 6
traveling, 36
Tyvek, 28
UPS, 35
use, 13
    beard guard, 14
    bed, 13
    display, 16
value, 30
washability test, 11
washing, 21
    bathtub, 24
    chlorine-free, 22
    machine, 22
Wright, Jeananne, 14, 15, 16, 18, 25, 28, 29, 42
Wyoming State Quilt Guild, 42

Author

Barb Gorges pieced and tied her first quilt in 1979 and switched to hand quilting for her fifth quilt in 1982. She tried machine quilting in 1980 for her third quilt, but didn't add it to her quilting methods until 1988 for project number 93.

She began teaching quilting in 1985 at the Custer County Art Center in Miles City, Montana, then through the continuing education department at Laramie County Community College in Cheyenne, Wyoming. Between 1995 and 2007, in addition to a variety of other classes, Barb taught 341 women (and one man) basic quilt making.

Barb's ribbons come from local and state competitions and a judge's choice at the National Quilting Association annual show. Two quilts have been juried into the American Quilter's Society show in Paducah, Kentucky. One was exhibited at Houston and two have travelled with the Original Sewing and Quilt Expo. Many of her quilts have become favorite objects of babies and other friends and family members.

By 1998, Barb's concern that non-quilters receiving quilts as gifts might not know how to care for them gave her the idea for the Gorges Quilt Care Label. She is happy to think that as many as 97,000 quilts in the U.S., Canada, Scotland, and Australia may have longer lives because they have a care label sewn on them.

Already a columnist for her local newspaper writing about birds and gardening, Barb decided to distill her knowledge of how to help quilts live to 100 into a series of essays published on her Gorges Quilt Labels blog, https://gorgesquiltcarelabels.com/, and then in the Wyoming State Quilt Guild newsletter. This book is based on them.

Barb enjoys the Wyoming outdoors with her husband, family and friends as often as possible.

www.ingramcontent.com/pod-product-compliance
Lightning Source LLC
Chambersburg PA
CBHW050448010526
44118CB00013B/1735